# PRINCEWILL LAGANG

# Marrying Right: A Christian's Guide to Choosing a Spouse

# Contents

1

# The Quest for a Godly Union

Title: Marrying Right: A Christian's Guide to Choosing a Spouse

The evening sun cast a warm, golden glow over the tranquil garden. As birds sang their melodious hymns and the scent of blooming flowers filled the air, Sarah found herself lost in thought. She sat on a weathered wooden bench, her Bible resting on her lap, contemplating the journey that lay ahead. In this moment of serenity, the idea of choosing a life partner seemed like a daunting adventure. But she knew she was on a quest—a quest to marry right, guided by her Christian faith.

Marrying right was a profound and sacred aspiration, a path that would lead to a lifetime of joy, love, and spiritual growth. It was an endeavor that required careful thought, discernment, and unwavering faith in God's divine plan.

The Sacred Institution of Marriage

As Christians, we are called to uphold the sanctity of marriage. In Ephesians 5:31, the apostle Paul reminds us, "For this reason, a man will leave his father and mother and be united to his wife, and the two will become one flesh." This verse reflects the divine purpose of marriage—a union where two souls become one in the eyes of God.

Christian marriage is more than a legal contract or a social arrangement; it is a covenant made before God. It is a reflection of Christ's love for His church. This profound spiritual connection requires us to approach the journey of choosing a spouse with reverence and faith. In doing so, we ensure that our union mirrors the love, commitment, and grace of Christ.

The Weight of the Decision

Selecting a life partner is perhaps the most crucial decision a Christian will make. It is a decision that carries lasting consequences, affecting not only your earthly life but also your spiritual journey. The person you choose to marry can either help you draw nearer to God or pull you away from Him.

Choosing a spouse is not an endeavor to be taken lightly. In 2 Corinthians 6:14, we are cautioned, "Do not be unequally yoked with unbelievers. For what partnership has righteousness with lawlessness? Or what fellowship has light with darkness?" This admonition underscores the importance of selecting a partner who shares your faith and values.

A Guide to Choosing Wisely

In this book, we will explore the principles and wisdom that can help you navigate the intricate path of choosing a spouse as a Christian. We will delve into the qualities to seek in a potential partner, the red flags to watch for, and the role of prayer and discernment in the decision-making process.

Our journey begins with self-reflection. Before seeking a life partner, it is essential to understand who you are, your values, and your relationship with God. The stronger your personal foundation, the better equipped you will be to discern a suitable spouse.

As we embark on this adventure together, remember that your heart's desire to marry right is in line with God's plan for your life. Trust in His guidance, seek wisdom from His word, and open your heart to His will. In doing so, you are well on your way to making one of the most important decisions of your life—one that will honor Him and bless you in ways beyond your wildest dreams.

In the following chapters, we will explore the qualities of a godly spouse, the importance of compatibility, and the role of faith in building a strong foundation for a Christ-centered marriage. So, let us embark on this sacred journey of "Marrying Right: A Christian's Guide to Choosing a Spouse" with faith, hope, and a heart open to God's divine plan.

# 2

# The Qualities of a Godly Spouse

Title: Marrying Right: A Christian's Guide to Choosing a Spouse

Sarah returned to the garden bench the following afternoon, her Bible in hand, her heart open to learning more about the qualities she should seek in a potential spouse. With the dappled sunlight illuminating the pages of Scripture, she knew that understanding the traits of a godly spouse was essential to her quest to marry right.

The Virtues of a Godly Spouse

In your pursuit of a Christ-centered marriage, it is crucial to consider the virtues and qualities that characterize a godly spouse. These qualities are not only desirable but necessary for a successful, fulfilling, and enduring marriage that aligns with God's will.

1. Faithfulness: At the core of a godly spouse is unwavering faith in God. This faith extends to their commitment to you as well. Look for someone who remains steadfast in their relationship with God, who keeps their promises, and who is devoted to the principles of fidelity and loyalty.

2. Love and Kindness: A godly spouse should embody the love and kindness

exemplified by Christ. They should show love not only in words but also in actions. Seek a partner who is compassionate, caring, and willing to extend grace and forgiveness.

3. Humility: In Philippians 2:3-4, we are reminded, "Do nothing out of selfish ambition or vain conceit. Rather, in humility, value others above yourselves, not looking to your own interests but each of you to the interests of the others." A godly spouse should possess humility, putting the needs of their partner ahead of their own.

4. Patience: A Christ-centered marriage requires patience, as love "is patient and kind" (1 Corinthians 13:4). Look for a partner who is willing to persevere through challenges, understanding that God's timing is perfect.

5. Respect: Mutual respect is essential in a Christian marriage. Seek someone who respects your opinions, values, and personal boundaries, just as you respect theirs.

6. Self-Control: A godly spouse exercises self-control in their actions and words. This quality ensures that conflicts are resolved with grace and that emotions do not overshadow reason.

7. Wisdom: Seek a partner who seeks wisdom from God and who makes decisions based on biblical principles. A wise spouse can provide valuable guidance in navigating the complexities of life.

8. A Shared Vision: Ensure that your potential spouse shares your vision for a Christ-centered life. Discuss your dreams, goals, and aspirations, both individually and as a couple, to make sure you are aligned in your pursuit of God's will.

The Fruit of the Spirit

In Galatians 5:22-23, the apostle Paul describes the fruit of the Spirit: love, joy, peace, patience, kindness, goodness, faithfulness, gentleness, and self-control. These virtues serve as a profound guide for what to seek in a godly spouse.

As you consider these qualities, remember that no one is perfect. Seek someone who is striving to embody these virtues and who is open to growth and transformation through their relationship with God. A godly spouse is not merely one who possesses these traits but is also committed to nurturing and expressing them daily.

Reflect and Pray

Take some time to reflect on the qualities you seek in a godly spouse. Write them down, and use them as a guide in your search. Share your desires with God in prayer, asking for His guidance in finding a partner who reflects His love and grace.

In the next chapter, we will explore compatibility and how these virtues and qualities play a crucial role in building a strong and lasting marriage founded on faith and love. As you continue your journey to marry right, remember that the qualities you seek in a spouse are a reflection of the love and grace you seek in your own heart.

# 3

# Compatibility and Building a Christ-Centered Marriage

Title: Marrying Right: A Christian's Guide to Choosing a Spouse

In the heart of the garden, Sarah continued her journey of seeking God's guidance in choosing a spouse. As she gazed upon the blooming flowers and listened to the melodious bird songs, she contemplated the importance of compatibility in building a Christ-centered marriage. The qualities of a godly spouse, explored in the previous chapter, were the foundation, but compatibility would be the cornerstone of a lifelong partnership.

Compatibility in Christ

In Corinthians 6:15, we are reminded that "what partnership has righteousness with lawlessness? Or what fellowship has light with darkness?" This verse underscores the importance of compatibility in faith, values, and life goals when seeking a life partner as a Christian. Compatibility in Christ is the first and most crucial aspect to consider.

1. Shared Faith: Seek a partner whose faith aligns with yours. A shared

commitment to Christ and His teachings will form the basis of your spiritual connection and help you grow together in your walk with God.

2. Common Values: Consider your core values and moral principles. A compatible spouse will share your values, ensuring that you both approach life's challenges and decisions from a similar ethical standpoint.

3. Spiritual Goals: Discuss your spiritual goals and aspirations. A compatible spouse will support your journey towards deepening your relationship with God and help you pursue His plan for your lives together.

Complementary Differences

While compatibility in faith and values is crucial, it's important to remember that differences also play a valuable role in building a Christ-centered marriage.

1. Complementary Strengths: A compatible partner may possess strengths and abilities that complement your own. This balance can lead to a harmonious and supportive partnership.

2. Challenges and Growth: Differences can also serve as opportunities for personal and spiritual growth. Challenges in your relationship can be transformative, drawing you closer to God and to each other.

Communication and Conflict Resolution

Effective communication and conflict resolution are fundamental to building a lasting marriage. A compatible spouse should be someone with whom you can openly and respectfully communicate.

1. Active Listening: Seek a partner who is an active listener and who values your perspective. This quality fosters understanding and empathy, allowing

you to resolve conflicts and disagreements with grace.

2. Conflict Resolution: A compatible spouse is someone who approaches conflict with a commitment to resolve it peacefully. Both of you should be willing to forgive and extend grace, mirroring God's love and forgiveness.

Shared Interests and Hobbies

While not all interests need to be identical, shared hobbies and activities can strengthen your bond. Look for common interests that you both enjoy, as they can provide opportunities for quality time together and mutual enjoyment.

Building a Christ-Centered Marriage

Compatibility is not solely about common interests and shared values; it's also about your commitment to God's plan for your marriage.

1. Prayer and Devotion: A Christ-centered marriage involves regular prayer and devotion together. Seek a spouse who shares your commitment to seeking God's guidance and strength.

2. Church and Community: Active involvement in your church and Christian community can strengthen your faith and your bond as a couple. Look for someone who values these connections.

3. Servant's Heart: Seek a partner who has a servant's heart, one who is willing to love and serve you as Christ did for His church. This selflessness is at the core of a Christ-centered marriage.

In Closing

As you consider compatibility, remember that it is an ongoing process. Your relationship will evolve as you grow individually and together in your faith.

Embrace the journey of building a Christ-centered marriage with an open heart and a steadfast commitment to God's plan.

In the next chapter, we will explore the vital role of prayer and discernment in the process of choosing a spouse. Through seeking God's guidance, you will continue on the path of marrying right and building a strong, enduring Christ-centered marriage.

# 4

# The Role of Prayer and Discernment

Title: Marrying Right: A Christian's Guide to Choosing a Spouse

The sun was beginning to set in the garden as Sarah sat in contemplation, her heart and mind focused on the critical role of prayer and discernment in her quest to marry right. With her Bible open before her and the soothing sounds of nature surrounding her, she knew that seeking God's guidance was paramount in choosing a life partner.

The Power of Prayer

Prayer is the cornerstone of seeking God's will in your life, especially when it comes to choosing a spouse. As Christians, prayer connects us with God and allows us to seek His guidance, wisdom, and direction in all aspects of our lives.

1. Prayer for Clarity: Begin by praying for clarity in your search for a spouse. Ask God to help you discern His will and to reveal the right person in His time.

2. Prayer for Wisdom: Seek God's wisdom in identifying the qualities and virtues you desire in a spouse. Pray for insight and understanding of His plan for your future.

3. Prayer for Patience: Waiting for the right partner can be challenging, but patience is a virtue. Pray for patience to trust God's timing in this important decision.

4. Prayer for Guidance: Ask God for guidance in your interactions with potential partners. Pray for discernment in recognizing whether someone aligns with His plan for your life.

Listening to God's Voice

Discernment involves listening to God's voice and understanding His direction. It is a process of deep reflection, self-examination, and seeking clarity on whether a person is the one God intends for you.

1. Inner Peace: Pay attention to your inner peace when considering a potential spouse. If you have a sense of peace about the relationship and believe it aligns with God's will, it may be a positive sign.

2. Alignment with Values: Reflect on whether the person shares your faith, values, and vision for a Christ-centered life. Do their beliefs and actions reflect a commitment to God's plan?

3. Community Input: Seek the counsel of trusted friends, family, and spiritual mentors who can offer guidance and insights. Sometimes, an outside perspective can help confirm God's direction.

4. Openness to Change: Be willing to change your plans if God's guidance points in a different direction. A spirit of openness to God's will is essential in discernment.

God's Timing Is Perfect

It's important to remember that God's timing is perfect. Waiting for the right person may require patience and trust in His plan.

1. Avoiding Impulsive Decisions: Resist the temptation to rush into a relationship out of loneliness or desperation. Trust that God has the perfect timing for your life.

2. Embracing Singleness: Use your season of singleness as an opportunity for personal and spiritual growth. Seek to deepen your relationship with God and become the best version of yourself.

Continual Prayer and Discernment

Prayer and discernment are not a one-time event but a continual process throughout your journey of seeking a spouse. As you navigate potential relationships and explore the possibility of marriage, maintain open communication with God through prayer.

1. Praying as a Couple: If you find someone you believe may be the one, pray together as a couple. Seek God's guidance in your relationship, asking for His blessings and direction.

2. Reflecting Together: Engage in open, honest conversations with your partner about your individual and shared spiritual journeys. Continual reflection together will help you grow closer to God and to each other.

In Closing

Prayer and discernment are essential elements in the process of choosing a spouse as a Christian. By staying connected to God through prayer and seeking His wisdom through discernment, you will find the guidance and direction you need to make one of the most significant decisions of your life.

In the next chapter, we will explore the practical aspects of dating, courtship, and building a strong foundation for a Christ-centered marriage. Through the lens of faith and guided by God's wisdom, you will be better equipped to marry right and embark on a lifelong journey of love, faith, and purpose.

5

# Navigating Dating and Courtship with Faith

Title: Marrying Right: A Christian's Guide to Choosing a Spouse

The garden's serene beauty was a fitting backdrop for Sarah's reflections on the practical aspects of dating and courtship from a Christian perspective. As she continued her journey to marry right, she recognized that the way she approached dating and courtship should align with her faith and values.

Dating with Purpose

Dating is a social activity that often leads to romantic relationships, but as a Christian, it should also serve a higher purpose: seeking a life partner who shares your faith and values. Here are some principles to guide you in dating with purpose:

1. Prayerful Beginnings: Start your dating journey with prayer, seeking God's guidance and wisdom. Pray for discernment to recognize whether the person you're considering aligns with God's plan for your life.

2. Purity and Boundaries: Maintain a commitment to purity in your dating relationship. Set physical and emotional boundaries to protect your purity and to honor God in your actions.

3. Shared Values: Use dating as an opportunity to understand the other person's values, faith, and vision for a Christ-centered life. Open and honest conversations can reveal the depth of your compatibility.

4. Community Involvement: Include trusted friends and family in your dating experience. Seek their counsel and guidance to ensure that your relationship reflects Christian principles.

Courtship: A Path to Marriage

Courtship is a more intentional and serious phase of a relationship, often with the goal of marriage in mind. It builds on the principles of dating with purpose and takes your commitment to a deeper level:

1. Seeking God's Will: Engage in courtship with the shared goal of seeking God's will for your relationship. Be open to the idea of marriage and take time to pray and discern together.

2. Accountability: Maintain accountability in your courtship. Continue to involve your community and spiritual mentors in your relationship to ensure it remains God-honoring.

3. Building a Spiritual Foundation: Use courtship to deepen your spiritual connection. Attend church together, read the Bible, and engage in prayer as a couple. A strong spiritual foundation is essential for a Christ-centered marriage.

4. Premarital Counseling: Consider premarital counseling to help you prepare for the challenges and joys of marriage. It provides valuable insights

and guidance for a strong, enduring partnership.

Red Flags and Warning Signs

As you navigate the realms of dating and courtship, it's important to be aware of red flags and warning signs that may indicate a relationship is not in alignment with God's will. These may include:

1. Conflict Resolution Styles: Pay attention to how conflicts are handled. A partner who avoids resolving issues, resorts to manipulation, or exhibits abusive behavior is not aligned with God's principles.

2. Differing Values: If you encounter significant differences in core values or faith, it may be a sign that the relationship isn't compatible with your Christian beliefs.

3. Lack of Accountability: If your partner resists or avoids involving your community in the relationship, it can be a sign of secrecy or an unwillingness to seek God's guidance.

In Closing

Dating and courtship are integral parts of the journey to finding the right spouse as a Christian. By dating with purpose, engaging in courtship with a commitment to God's will, and being vigilant about red flags, you can navigate these stages of a relationship while remaining faithful to your Christian values.

In the next chapter, we will explore the process of engagement and preparing for a Christ-centered marriage. As you continue to seek God's guidance and remain committed to His plan, you will be well on your way to marrying right and building a strong, lifelong partnership.

6

# Engagement and Preparing for a Christ-Centered Marriage

Title: Marrying Right: A Christian's Guide to Choosing a Spouse

As Sarah ventured further along her path to marrying right, she contemplated the significance of the engagement period. This time of commitment, preparation, and anticipation held the promise of a Christ-centered marriage, and it was essential to approach it with faith and diligence.

The Purpose of Engagement

Engagement is a unique phase in a relationship. It signifies the intention to marry and provides an opportunity for deeper preparation and connection as a couple:

1. Spiritual Preparation: Engage in pre-marital counseling and spiritual reflection. This period should be a time of strengthening your spiritual connection and readiness for the covenant of marriage.

2. Planning the Wedding: As you plan your wedding, ensure it reflects your Christian values and priorities. Seek a ceremony and celebration that honor

God's role in your relationship.

3. Public Commitment: Your engagement serves as a public declaration of your intent to marry. It allows your family and community to share in your joy and hold you accountable to your commitment.

4. Emotional and Practical Readiness: Use this time to discuss important matters such as your future home, family, and finances. Ensure you are both emotionally and practically ready for marriage.

Preparing for a Christ-Centered Marriage

A Christ-centered marriage is the goal for every Christian couple. Preparing for this type of partnership involves deliberate actions and choices:

1. Prayer and Devotion: Continue to pray together as a couple, seeking God's guidance for your marriage. Invest in spiritual growth through reading the Bible and attending church as one.

2. Open and Honest Communication: Communication is vital to the health of a marriage. Establish a foundation of open and honest communication during your engagement, which will serve you well throughout your marriage.

3. Conflict Resolution Skills: Strengthen your conflict resolution skills. Use the engagement period as an opportunity to address any unresolved issues and to practice resolving conflicts with grace and empathy.

4. Service and Sacrifice: Learn to serve and sacrifice for each other. A Christ-centered marriage is built on a foundation of selflessness and love, mirroring Christ's love for His church.

5. Financial Planning: Address financial matters together and ensure you are on the same page regarding budgeting, saving, and financial goals.

6. Future Goals: Continue discussing your future goals and vision for a Christ-centered life. Ensure your dreams align and that you both feel called to the same mission in life.

Seeking Counsel

Engagement is an opportune time to seek counsel and guidance from those with experience and wisdom:

1. Marriage Mentors: Consider finding a Christian couple or mentor who can provide guidance and support as you prepare for marriage. They can share their experiences and offer valuable insights.

2. Family and Friends: Involve your trusted friends and family in your preparations. Their prayers and advice can be invaluable.

Honoring God in Your Wedding

Your wedding is a sacred event that should reflect your Christian faith and values:

1. Select a God-Honoring Venue: Choose a venue that aligns with your faith and is conducive to a Christ-centered ceremony.

2. Scripture and Vows: Incorporate meaningful Bible verses and Christian vows into your ceremony. Let your love and commitment to each other be a testament to your love for God.

In Closing

Engagement is a sacred period of anticipation and preparation for a Christ-centered marriage. Approach it with faith, prayer, and a commitment to nurturing your spiritual connection. By preparing diligently and seeking counsel, you will be well-equipped to embark on your lifelong journey of love, faith, and purpose as you marry right.

7

# The Covenant of Marriage

Title: Marrying Right: A Christian's Guide to Choosing a Spouse

As Sarah stood at the threshold of her wedding day, the culmination of her journey to marry right, she marveled at the sacredness of the covenant of marriage. The serene garden seemed to echo the significance of this moment, and she understood that the commitment she was about to make was not to be taken lightly.

The Biblical Foundation of Marriage

The covenant of marriage is deeply rooted in the Bible, serving as a reflection of the relationship between Christ and His church:

1. Ephesians 5:25: "Husbands, love your wives, just as Christ loved the church and gave himself up for her." This verse underscores the sacrificial and selfless nature of a husband's love.

2. Proverbs 18:22: "He who finds a wife finds what is good and receives favor from the Lord." Marriage is viewed as a divine gift, bringing God's favor to those who enter into this covenant.

3. Genesis 2:24: "For this reason, a man will leave his father and mother and be united to his wife, and they will become one flesh." This verse reveals the oneness and unity that marriage creates.

The Sacred Vows

The exchange of vows is the heart of a Christian wedding. These vows are not mere words but solemn promises made before God and witnesses:

1. Love and Cherish: Vows to love, cherish, and honor one another mirror Christ's love for His church. They signify a commitment to care for, protect, and treasure your spouse.

2. For Better or Worse: Vows to be there in good times and bad times reflect the enduring nature of Christ's love. This commitment carries the couple through life's challenges, knowing that God's grace sustains them.

3. Faithfulness: Pledges of faithfulness are a promise to keep the marriage covenant sacred, just as Christ is unwavering in His love for the church.

The Role of God in Marriage

A Christ-centered marriage acknowledges God as the foundation and sustainer of the relationship:

1. Shared Faith: A shared faith in God is central to a Christian marriage. It is the source of strength, hope, and guidance.

2. Prayer and Devotion: Regular prayer and devotion as a couple are essential for maintaining a strong spiritual connection.

3. Grace and Forgiveness: A Christ-centered marriage is characterized by grace and forgiveness, mirroring Christ's forgiveness of His church.

Building a Strong Marriage

A strong Christian marriage is a continuous journey of growth and love:

1. Communication: Open and honest communication is the cornerstone of a strong marriage. It enables understanding and intimacy.

2. Conflict Resolution: Learning to resolve conflicts with grace and empathy strengthens the marriage. Seek to mirror God's love and forgiveness in your interactions.

3. Service and Sacrifice: Selflessness and service are the keys to a lasting and joyful marriage.

4. Community Support: Stay connected to your church and Christian community for support, guidance, and fellowship.

In Closing

The covenant of marriage is a profound and sacred commitment, a reflection of the love and grace of Christ for His church. As you embark on your marriage journey, keep God at the center, maintain open communication, and practice grace and forgiveness. By doing so, you will be well on your way to building a strong, enduring, and Christ-centered marriage, and you will have truly married right.

8

# Nurturing a Lifelong Christ-Centered Marriage

Title: Marrying Right: A Christian's Guide to Choosing a Spouse

As Sarah stood before the beautiful garden, now in the full bloom of her marriage, she reflected on the journey she and her spouse had embarked upon. Their wedding day was just the beginning, and she understood that nurturing a lifelong, Christ-centered marriage was a continuous process of growth, love, and faith.

The Ongoing Journey

A Christ-centered marriage is a journey that continues to evolve and deepen over time. It is not defined by the wedding day but by the commitment to walk hand in hand with faith:

1. Prayer and Devotion: Continue to nurture your spiritual connection through prayer and devotion as a couple. Your shared faith is the foundation of your marriage.

2. Communication: Maintain open and honest communication. Make

a commitment to continually deepen your understanding of each other's thoughts and feelings.

3. Conflict Resolution: Embrace conflict as an opportunity for growth. Practice resolving disagreements with grace and empathy, understanding that God's love and forgiveness guide your interactions.

4. Service and Sacrifice: Keep the spirit of selflessness alive in your marriage. Serving and sacrificing for one another is a reflection of Christ's love for His church.

5. Community Support: Stay connected to your church and Christian community. Seek their support, guidance, and fellowship throughout your marriage.

Love, Joy, and Purpose

A Christ-centered marriage is characterized by the love, joy, and purpose that are a reflection of God's grace:

1. Love: Continue to love one another deeply and unconditionally. Your love for your spouse should mirror Christ's love for His church.

2. Joy: Find joy in your marriage. Share moments of laughter, happiness, and contentment as you journey through life together.

3. Purpose: Embrace your shared purpose as a couple. Seek to fulfill God's plan for your lives, using your marriage as a means to achieve His purpose.

Caring for Your Marriage

Nurturing a Christ-centered marriage requires active care and attention:

1. Date Nights: Continue to prioritize spending quality time together. Date nights can help keep the romance and intimacy alive in your marriage.

2. Surprises and Affection: Surprise your spouse with gestures of affection and appreciation. Small acts of love can have a profound impact on your relationship.

3. Continual Growth: Both individually and as a couple, commit to continual growth. Pursue personal and spiritual development to strengthen your marriage.

4. Renewal: Periodically take time for renewal and reflection. Retreats, vacations, or simply quiet moments together can rejuvenate your connection.

In Times of Trial

A Christ-centered marriage may face its share of trials and challenges. Remember that God's grace is your anchor:

1. Seek God Together: In times of difficulty, turn to God in prayer together. Let your shared faith be a source of strength.

2. Counsel and Support: If necessary, seek marriage counseling from a trusted Christian professional who can provide guidance and support.

3. Never Give Up: Remember your vows to love and cherish each other, in good times and bad. Commit to working through difficulties and growing stronger in your marriage.

In Closing

Nurturing a lifelong, Christ-centered marriage is a rewarding and fulfilling journey. By maintaining a strong spiritual connection, practicing open communication, and demonstrating love and selflessness, you will continue to honor God in your partnership. Through the love and grace of Christ, your marriage will be a testament to faith, love, and purpose, proving that you have indeed married right.

9

# Passing Down a Legacy of Faith

Title: Marrying Right: A Christian's Guide to Choosing a Spouse

Years had passed since Sarah's wedding day in the tranquil garden, and she now found herself reflecting on the legacy of faith she and her spouse were building together. Their marriage had become a testament to the enduring love and grace of Christ, and they recognized the importance of passing down this legacy to future generations.

A Legacy of Faith

A Christ-centered marriage has the power to leave a profound legacy for your children and the generations that follow. Here are some key aspects to consider when passing down a legacy of faith:

1. Lead by Example: Your actions speak louder than words. Demonstrate your faith through your love, grace, and service to others. Show your children what it means to live out a Christian life.

2. Teach and Share: Take the time to teach your children about your faith. Share Bible stories, lessons, and the values that guide your life. Encourage their questions and provide thoughtful, age-appropriate answers.

3. Pray Together: Make prayer a family practice. Praying together fosters a sense of unity and reliance on God as a family.

4. Worship and Community: Attend church together as a family. Engage in your Christian community and encourage your children to develop their own relationships with God.

5. Service and Giving: Involve your children in acts of service and giving. Show them the importance of helping others and living out the love of Christ.

Creating Family Traditions

Family traditions can be a powerful way to pass down your faith and values:

1. Bible Study: Establish regular family Bible study or devotion times. Make it a tradition to explore Scripture together.

2. Holiday Celebrations: Infuse your holiday celebrations with Christian meaning. For example, incorporate Easter and Christmas traditions that emphasize the true reason for these holidays.

3. Family Meals: Use family meals as an opportunity for prayer, gratitude, and meaningful conversations about faith.

4. Mission Trips and Service: Plan family mission trips or service projects to help your children understand the importance of serving others.

Encouraging Independence

As your children grow, encourage them to develop their personal relationship with God:

1. Allow Questions: Be open to your children's questions about faith.

Encourage them to explore their beliefs and develop a personal understanding of God.

2. Provide Guidance: Offer guidance and mentorship as they navigate their own faith journey. Be a source of support and wisdom.

3. Respect Their Choices: While you hope your children will follow in your faith footsteps, respect their choices if they decide to explore other beliefs or spiritual paths. Continue to love and support them.

Staying Committed as a Couple

A strong and loving marriage is the foundation for passing down a legacy of faith:

1. Continue to Grow Spiritually: Maintain your own spiritual growth and commitment to your faith. Your example as a couple is a significant influence on your children.

2. Work Through Challenges Together: Facing challenges as a couple with grace and love demonstrates the strength and power of your faith.

3. Reconnect and Recharge: Periodically take time as a couple to reconnect and recharge your spiritual connection. Retreats, date nights, and quiet moments together can help you stay rooted in your faith.

In Closing

Passing down a legacy of faith is one of the most significant gifts you can give to your children and future generations. By leading by example, creating meaningful family traditions, and encouraging independence, you will ensure that your Christ-centered marriage becomes a lasting testament to God's love, grace, and purpose. In this way, you will have truly married right, not only for yourself but for the generations that follow.

# 10

# Embracing a Lifelong Journey of Love, Faith, and Purpose

Title: Marrying Right: A Christian's Guide to Choosing a Spouse

Sarah, now with decades of married life behind her, stood in the same garden where her journey had begun. As she looked back and forward, she understood that marrying right was not just a destination but a lifelong journey of love, faith, and purpose.

The Ongoing Commitment

A Christ-centered marriage is a lifelong commitment. It's a journey that encompasses all the chapters of your life:

1. Continual Growth: Embrace the journey of continual growth, both individually and as a couple. Your faith, love, and purpose should deepen with time.

2. Adapting to Change: Be prepared to adapt to life's changes and challenges. The strength of your faith and love will guide you through various seasons.

3. Support and Community: Stay connected to your Christian community and seek support from mentors, friends, and fellow believers. They will be there to encourage you on your journey.

Nurturing Your Love

Love is the core of your Christ-centered marriage. Nurturing it should be a lifelong pursuit:

1. Renewal of Love: Periodically renew your love for each other. Continue to date, surprise, and cherish one another.

2. Joy in Marriage: Find joy in your marriage every day. Laughter, shared moments, and small celebrations should be a part of your journey.

3. Service and Sacrifice: Keep the spirit of service and sacrifice alive. Loving your spouse as Christ loved the church remains the cornerstone of your marriage.

4. Evolving Intimacy: Intimacy in your marriage should evolve and deepen over time. Embrace the beauty of growing closer to each other as you grow closer to God.

Passing Down the Legacy

A lifelong journey of love, faith, and purpose should be a legacy that extends to your children and generations to come:

1. Lead by Example: Your life should be a testament to your faith and values, setting an example for your children and grandchildren.

2. Family Traditions: Continue to create and maintain family traditions that emphasize your faith and values. Pass down your commitment to God in a

tangible way.

3. Encourage Independence: Support your children as they develop their own relationship with God. Be a source of guidance, love, and wisdom as they navigate their faith journey.

Reflection and Renewal

Throughout your lifelong journey, moments of reflection and renewal are essential:

1. Retreats and Getaways: Periodically take time as a couple to retreat from the busyness of life. Reflect on your journey and renew your commitment to each other and God.

2. Spiritual Growth: Continue to grow spiritually as individuals and as a couple. Your faith journey should always be evolving.

3. Reconnect and Recharge: Regularly reconnect with your spouse. Date nights, quality time, and moments of deep connection are vital for maintaining the bond between you.

In Closing

Marrying right is not just about choosing the right spouse; it's about embarking on a lifelong journey of love, faith, and purpose. By nurturing your love, passing down a legacy of faith, and continually renewing your commitment, you ensure that your Christ-centered marriage will remain a powerful testament to God's love and grace. Your journey is an inspiring story of faith and love that will impact not only your life but the lives of those who follow in your footsteps.

# 11

# Conclusion - A Journey of Eternal Significance

Title: Marrying Right: A Christian's Guide to Choosing a Spouse

In the same serene garden where Sarah's journey had begun, she now stood at the end of the book's journey. This concluding chapter served as a reminder that the quest to marry right, guided by faith and love, is a journey of eternal significance. It's a journey that never truly ends, as its impact extends beyond this lifetime.

The Eternal Significance of Marriage

A Christ-centered marriage holds eternal significance, and it is a reflection of the divine relationship between Christ and His church:

1. Ephesians 5:32: "This is a profound mystery—but I am talking about Christ and the church." Your marriage, as a reflection of this profound mystery, carries eternal weight and significance.

2. A Witness to God's Love: Your marriage serves as a witness to the world of God's love and grace. It's a living testament to the beauty of a Christ-centered life.

The Legacy of Love

As you close this chapter of the book, it's essential to reflect on the legacy of love you are building in your marriage:

1. Eternal Impact: Your love, faith, and purpose have an eternal impact on your life, your spouse, your children, and even generations to come.

2. A Witness to Future Generations: Your marriage is a witness to your children and grandchildren, inspiring them to carry on the legacy of faith and love.

Reflection and Gratitude

Take time to reflect on your journey and express gratitude for the love, faith, and purpose that have guided your path:

1. Reflection: Consider the highs and lows, the joys and challenges, and the growth that you've experienced throughout your journey.

2. Gratitude: Express gratitude for the love of God, the grace of Christ, and the guidance of the Holy Spirit that have sustained your marriage.

3. A Prayer of Thanksgiving: Offer a prayer of thanksgiving for the journey you've embarked on and for the journey yet to come.

The Never-Ending Journey

While this book may come to a close, your journey of marrying right and living out a Christ-centered marriage is never-ending:

1. Continual Growth: Commit to ongoing growth, both individually and as a couple. Let your faith, love, and purpose deepen with time.

2. Embracing Change: Life will bring change and challenges. Embrace them with faith, knowing that your love and God's grace will guide you through.

3. Nurturing Your Love: Keep the love alive in your marriage. Nurture it, celebrate it, and let it be a light to the world.

4. Passing Down the Legacy: Continue to pass down the legacy of faith and love to your children and generations to come.

In Closing

The conclusion of this book marks the beginning of the rest of your lifelong journey. As you move forward, remember that marrying right is not a destination but a journey of eternal significance. With faith, love, and purpose as your guides, you are on a path that leads to a life filled with love, joy, and the enduring grace of Christ. Your journey is a story of eternal significance, a journey that you are privileged to undertake as you marry right and continue walking the path of love, faith, and purpose.

# 12

# Resources and Further Reading

Title: Marrying Right: A Christian's Guide to Choosing a Spouse

As you conclude this journey, you may be eager to explore additional resources and readings that can deepen your understanding of marrying right and maintaining a Christ-centered marriage. This chapter provides a selection of recommended resources to support your ongoing pursuit of love, faith, and purpose in your relationship.

Books on Christian Marriage:

1. "The Meaning of Marriage" by Timothy Keller: This book delves into the profound mysteries of marriage, exploring its purpose and significance in a Christian context.

2. "Sacred Marriage" by Gary Thomas: Gary Thomas offers unique insights into how marriage can be a spiritual discipline, helping you draw closer to God through your relationship.

3. "Love & Respect" by Dr. Emerson Eggerichs: Focused on the biblical

principle of husbands loving their wives and wives respecting their husbands, this book provides practical advice for a strong marriage.

Devotional and Study Guides:

4. "The Love Dare" by Stephen and Alex Kendrick: Based on the popular movie "Fireproof," this devotional challenges couples to strengthen their love and faith.

5. "The Love and Respect Experience" by Dr. Emerson Eggerichs: This devotional helps couples apply the principles from "Love & Respect" to their daily lives.

6. "The Power of a Praying Wife" and "The Power of a Praying Husband" by Stormie Omartian: These devotionals offer guidance on how to pray for your spouse and deepen your spiritual connection.

Marriage Counseling and Support:

7. Focus on the Family: Their website (focusonthefamily.com) offers a wealth of resources, articles, and tools for strengthening your marriage.

8. MarriageToday: Founded by Jimmy and Karen Evans, MarriageToday provides practical insights and resources to build a strong, Christ-centered marriage (marriagetoday.com).

Christian Marriage Seminars and Workshops:

9. Weekend to Remember: Hosted by FamilyLife, this weekend marriage conference provides practical tools and biblical wisdom to strengthen your marriage (familylife.com/weekend-to-remember).

10. Love and Respect Conferences: Based on Dr. Emerson Eggerichs'

principles, these conferences offer in-depth guidance on building a loving and respectful marriage (loveandrespect.com).

Christian Marriage Blogs and Online Communities:

11. Marriage Missions International: This website offers a wealth of articles, resources, and advice for couples seeking to strengthen their Christian marriages (marriagemissions.com).

12. The Generous Wife and The Generous Husband: These two blogs provide daily tips and advice for married couples looking to deepen their connection and faith (generouswife.com and generoushusband.com).

Additional Reading on Parenting and Passing Down Your Faith:

13. "Spiritual Parenting" by Michelle Anthony: This book explores how to pass down your faith to your children and create a spiritually rich family life.

14. "Parenting with Love and Logic" by Charles Fay and Foster Cline: While not explicitly Christian, this book offers practical parenting advice that aligns with Christian principles.

These resources will serve as valuable companions on your ongoing journey of love, faith, and purpose in your Christian marriage. Whether you are newlyweds or have been married for decades, there is always room to grow in your relationship with God and your spouse. May your journey be filled with love, grace, and enduring faith as you continue to marry right and build a Christ-centered marriage.

Title: Marrying Right: A Christian's Guide to Choosing a Spouse

Book Summary:

"Marrying Right: A Christian's Guide to Choosing a Spouse" is a comprehensive guide that takes readers on a journey through the principles, wisdom, and faith-based insights essential for building a Christ-centered marriage. This book is a practical resource for individuals seeking to find the right spouse and cultivate a relationship firmly grounded in Christian values.

The book is divided into twelve chapters, each addressing a different aspect of the journey to marry right. It covers topics such as understanding one's own readiness for marriage, seeking God's guidance in choosing a spouse, navigating the dating and courtship process with faith, and preparing for a Christ-centered marriage through engagement. It also explores the importance of nurturing love, passing down a legacy of faith to future generations, and continually growing in one's Christian marriage.

Throughout the book, readers will find insightful guidance on key issues, including setting boundaries, resolving conflicts with grace and empathy, and building a strong spiritual foundation for a lasting marriage. The author emphasizes the significance of maintaining an open and honest line of communication and the importance of seeking guidance from trusted mentors and the Christian community.

The book underlines that a Christ-centered marriage is not just a goal but a continuous journey. It is a lifelong commitment, with the love and grace of Christ at its core. It explores the eternal significance of marriage and its role as a reflection of the divine relationship between Christ and His church, emphasizing that a Christ-centered marriage can impact generations to come.

In the final chapter, the book provides a list of recommended resources, including books on Christian marriage, devotional and study guides, marriage counseling and support organizations, marriage seminars and workshops, blogs, and online communities. These resources are intended to help readers continue their journey of love, faith, and purpose in their Christian marriage.

"Marrying Right: A Christian's Guide to Choosing a Spouse" is an invaluable guide for individuals seeking to build strong, enduring, and Christ-centered marriages.  It serves as a source of inspiration, guidance, and wisdom for those on a path to marrying right and living a life of love, faith, and purpose.

www.ingramcontent.com/pod-product-compliance
Lightning Source LLC
LaVergne TN
LVHW041245200726
843507LV00013B/2816